SUMMARY & ANALYSIS

OF

THE Clean 20

20 Foods, 20 Days, Total Transformation

A GUIDE TO THE BOOK
BY IAN K. SMITH, M.D.

NOTE: This book is a summary and analysis and is meant as a companion to, not a replacement for, the original book.

Please follow this link to purchase a copy of the original book: https://amzn.to/2KuhwYG

TABLE OF CONTENTS

SYNOPSIS

Dr. Ian K. Smith's, *The Clean 20: 20 Foods, 20 Days, Total Transformation* is part diet book, part motivational book, part cookbook, and part nutritional guide. The book is broken down into three simple sections. The first reviews in detail the 20 foods that Smith recommends along with nutritional content, tips for purchasing produce, and even some history of lesser-known grains. The guide is comprehensive and provides insight into why he has chosen each of these foods.

The second section shifts to more practical matters, breaking down the specific rules of the diet and offering some guidelines for success. The second section will also be your daily guide as you move through the 20-day program, containing detailed daily meal plans with everything from recipes and suggested exercises to a daily motivational theme.

The final section is devoted completely to Smith's recipes, which utilize all of the Clean 20 ingredients (and then some) to provide delicious, well-balanced meal options for anyone attempting to follow the plan. In addition, he provides instructions on how to perform each of the exercises mentioned in his suggestions for daily activity. Overall, the book is simple, easy-to-follow, and well-organized.

WHAT IS CLEAN EATING?

The concept of clean eating has gained more and more traction in the past few years, but what does it mean exactly? With raw diets, paleo diets, and gluten-free diets, what constitutes a clean diet? Dr. Ian K. Smith suggests clean eating is simply eating more natural and fewer processed foods: fewer burgers, more vegetables. He argues, rightly so, that this is both good for your body and for the environment.

Clean eating, however, does not mean never eating anything processed (that would be extremely difficult), and he is sure to point out that processed doesn't necessarily mean something is terrible for you. There are specific things you should be actively looking out for and actively trying to avoid in order to follow a clean diet. Generally speaking, food items with more than five ingredients listed probably don't fall under the "clean eating" umbrella. Additionally, you must focus on eating nutrient-dense foods: foods with high concentrations of nutrients, but low calorie counts, such as vegetables. The more that what's on your plate looks like the thing that came out of the ground, the cleaner you're eating.

Key Takeaway: Not all processed foods are evil.

While avoiding overly processed foods or foods with more than five ingredients is a good place to start, there are plenty of "processed" foods that aren't bad for you. For example, all flour is processed from grains. This doesn't make it inherently bad, but there are specific types of processed grains you want to avoid.

If a grain is refined, it means that much of its nutrients have been stripped out. Look for "100% whole grain" or "100% whole wheat." And don't be fooled by "multi-grain." This can often just mean several refined, over-processed grains are added together.

Key Takeaway: Sugar isn't evil, but added sugar is.

As most people are already aware, sugar occurs naturally in many foods. You may be thinking of apples and oranges, but sugar also occurs naturally in plenty of vegetables such as peppers, carrots, corn, potatoes and squash. There is no diet that would recommend removing ALL sugar from the diet; it's removing ADDED sugars that leads to clean eating.

Added sugars make up at least 10% of the calories the average American eats in a day, and up to 25% for some. Diets with the most added sugar lead to serious health complications, such as diabetes and heart disease, and decreased life span over time. Sugar is added to almost everything we see in the grocery store today, even products you don't consider sweet. Cakes, soda, and juice have added sugar, but often so do crackers, salad dressings, mayonnaise, and other savory products that would surprise you. This is because sugar is addictive; it causes you to feel hungry again faster and want to eat more food. The more you eat, the more money food corporations make; thus, they have an incentive to sneak it into as many products as possible.

Be sure to check nutrition labels for added sugars that could be hiding under many different names like dextrose, maltrose, fructose, glucitol, and hexitol. Note the suffixes on these names: -ose and -itol. These are commonly associated with processed, added sugars.

Key Takeaway: Avoid food additives when possible.

Processed foods are filled with additives such as food coloring and preservatives. Most of what we eat we wouldn't recognize without the dyes such as Blue No. 1 and Red No. 40. Xanthan gum is commonly added to stabilize things like pudding and salad dressings, and there is a long list of preservatives used to stop food from spoiling. While preservatives like salt have been used for centuries to keep meat and fish fresh for longer, some of the modern ones, like MSG, may have unintended health consequences. Though food without preservatives will often spoil faster, you can still balance your shopping to avoid having to make multiple trips to the store each week.

THE CLEAN 20 FOODS

Dr. Smith's plan consists of switching to a clean diet of 20 specified foods for 20 days. He is careful to mention that you don't have to follow his list of 20 foods exactly. You may substitute any foods you like, so long as they meet the criteria for clean eating.

Below is an overview from the book of the benefits of various vitamins and minerals that are found in the Clean 20 foods:

CLEAN 20 Minerals	
Calcium	Makes bones and teeth; helps with muscle contraction/relaxation, nerve function, blood clotting, and blood pressure maintenance.
Chromium	Helps insulin move glucose from the blood into the cells.
Copper	Aids digestion and absorption; lubricates joints and organs; regulates body temperature.
Iodine	Component of thyroid hormone—regulates growth, development, and metabolism.
Iron	Part of hemoglobin molecule; carries oxygen in the blood.
Magnesium	Helps with mineralization of bones and teeth, muscle contraction, nerve conduction, enzyme function.
Phosphorus	Helps maintain bones and teeth; important in our DNA and cell membranes; helps body get energy from food.
Selenium	Antioxidant that works with vitamin E and fights damaging particles in the body called free radicals.
Sodium	Controls fluid balance; assists nerve impulse transmission and muscle contractions.
Zinc	Helps many enzymes function properly; part of insulin molecule; helps DNA repair as well as immune function, wound healing, and taste perception.

CLEAN 20 Vitamins	
Vitamin A (Retinol)	Improves eyesight; helps with bone growth and reproduction; regulates immune system; helps with appetite and taste.
Vitamin B1 (Thiamine)	Part of enzyme needed for energy metabolism; important for nerve, muscle, and heart function as well as digestion.
Vitamin B2 (Riboflavin)	Important for normal vision and skin health as well as nails and eyesight; helps with breakdown of fat and carbohydrates.
Vitamin B3 (Niacin)	Important for digestive system, nervous system, and skin health.
Vitamin B5 (Pantothenic Acid)	Plays a role in the breakdown of fats and carbohydrates for energy; important for manufacture of red blood cells as well as sex and stress-related hormones produced in adrenal glands.
Vitamin B6 (Pyridoxine)	Needed for protein metabolism; helps make red blood cells and prevent nerve and skin conditions.
Vitamin B9 (Folic Acid)	Part of an enzyme needed for making DNA and new cells, particularly red blood cells; essential in first three months of pregnancy to prevent spina bifida, cleft palate, and cleft lip.
Vitamin B12 (Cobalamin)	Needed for making new cells; important to nerve function.
Vitamin C (Ascorbic Acid)	Antioxidant that fights toxins; part of an enzyme needed for protein metabolism; helps with iron absorption; important for immune system health.
Vitamin D	Needed for proper absorption of calcium; important for strong bones and teeth.
Vitamin E (Tocopherol)	Antioxidant that fights toxins; protects cell wall from damage; supports immune function and DNA repair.
Vitamin K	Need for the blood to clot properly.

Image Credit: Smith, Ian K., M.D.. The Clean 20: 20 Foods, 20 Days, Total Transformation (pp. 14-15). St. Martin's Press. Kindle Edition.

After reviewing the essential vitamins and minerals your clean diet should be providing, Smith provides a detailed list of recommend foods along with "basket buddies," or foods you can use to replace the original suggestion. For example, he lists "berries," but the basket buddies are apples, pears, mangos, and bananas, among others. If you don't want berries as one of your clean 20, you may substitute any of the basket buddies in its place. For each food listed below, Smith provides an in-depth picture of its nutrients and health benefits, along with some history of the food and tips for shopping. Foods are presented in alphabetical order.

Avocado

· At 75% fat, the avocado is the fattiest fruit on the list

· The fats in avocados are monounsaturated, meaning they are good for your cholesterol levels

· Chock full of nutrients including vitamins B5, folate, K, B6, and E, and they possess antioxidant and anti-inflammatory properties

· Avocados are delicious, full of flavor, and can be sliced on a salad or spread on a piece of toast

Blueberries, Raspberries, and Strawberries

· Low in calories, but bursting with nutrients

· Typically rich in antioxidants, which can help fight the aging process as well as the onset of disease

· Significant source of vitamins such as Vitamins A, B-complex, C, and K, along with minerals like iron, selenium, and zinc

· Berries are a little-known source of dietary fiber—one of the most important components of clean eating

Cheese

· A great source of vitamin A, calcium, and a particular protein rich in amino acids known as casein

· "The healthiest cheeses on the planet" are cottage cheese, feta, mozzarella, parmesan, and ricotta

- You can also use classics like swiss, American, and cheddar

"Simply put, calcium is the most abundant mineral in our body and we need lots of it to stay healthy." (Smith, p. 24).

Chicken

- Chicken is both an excellent source of protein and a super-lean meat
- Also a great source of vitamin B3, selenium, phosphorus, and choline
- Chicken is extremely versatile in how it can be cooked
- Roasting and frying are the least healthy methods and are *not* part of the Clean 20 plan
- "Pasture" or "Pasture-Raised" chicken is the best label to look for in the store, though "naturally raised," "free-range," and "organic" are also desirable
- All chickens labeled "organic" must be "free-range," but not all "free-range" chickens must be "organic"

Chickpeas, aka Garbanzo Beans

- Of Middle Eastern origin, this flavorful and versatile legume is known for its nutty flavor and buttery texture
- Inexpensive, high in nutrition, and low in calories

- High in fiber, good source of protein, folate, zinc, and antioxidants

- If buying canned chickpeas, check to make sure the sodium content isn't too high

- Great in soups, salads, mashed, roasted as a snack, or spread on pita

Eggs

- Eggs contain some of almost every nutrient we need, and are extremely affordable

- Cholesterol and eggs is a myth: our body uses the cholesterol we consume from eggs, and eggs may even help reduce levels of unhealthy LDL cholesterols

- The standards for humane egg production vary, but "Certified Humane," "Animal Welfare Approved," "Cage-Free," and "Certified Organic" will all be better than the cheapest, factory-farmed eggs available

Kale

- In place of kale, you can substitute arugula, bok choy, brussels sprouts, cabbage, cauliflower, collard greens, spinach, or swiss chard

- Kale contains 45 different antioxidant polyphenols

- Rich in vitamins K, A, B1, B2, E, and C

- Also provides manganese, copper, carotenoids, and protein

Lemons

- A great source of vitamin C with far fewer calories than an orange
- Contains vitamins A, C, B6, E, folate, and riboflavin as well as copper, calcium, iron, and magnesium
- Many medicinal properties including soothing sore throats, suppressing appetite, reducing fever and cold symptoms, and they are also a diuretic
- Add the juice of half a lemon to your glass of water for a big vitamin and mineral boost with very few calories

Lentils

- Can be substituted with black beans, green beans, kidney beans, white beans, or soybeans, but lentils are best
- Lentils are powerhouses in the legume family stuffed full of protein, fiber, and vitamins—notably B-complex vitamins
- Lentils can improve heart health, digestion, diabetes, and atherosclerosis
- Very inexpensive and easy to cook in soups, or add to salads and wraps

Nuts and Seeds

- Almond, cashews, pecans, pine nuts, pistachios, pumpkin seeds, sunflower seeds, and walnuts are best

- Not eating enough nuts and seeds is the third leading dietary risk factor for death and disability in the world

- While most nuts have similar health properties, walnuts are slightly better than all the rest containing more antioxidants and omega-3 fatty acids

- Be sure to choose raw nuts, and not nuts that have been processed with sugar or artificial ingredients; lightly salted is ok

Oatmeal

- Oatmeal is a truly whole grain—it contains the bran, the endosperm, and the germ—parts of which are usually lost during refining and processing

- Steel-cut oats are the least processed option you will find in the grocery store; old-fashioned rolled oats and Scottish oats are also fine, but quick or instant rolled oats are the most processed variety

Quinoa

- Quinoa is neither a true grain nor a cereal grass; it is an edible seed that is also gluten-free and high in protein

- Considered a super-food, it contains fiber, folate, iron, calcium, zinc, omega-3 fatty acids, and is a "complete protein," meaning it provides all nine of the essential amino acids our bodies need

- Quinoa is believed to aid in reducing the risk of many diseases such as diabetes, cardiovascular disease, obesity, and colon cancer

Seafood

- Most seafood is good, but your best options are cod, crab, halibut, lobster, oysters, salmon, sea bass, shrimp, and tuna

- It is recommended to eat seafood at least twice a week

- Fish are full of protein, vitamins D & A (among others), and rich in minerals and essential Omega-3 fatty acids that our bodies can't produce in large enough quantities on their own

- Wild-caught fish is always best, but farm-raised may still be ok; be aware of mercury levels

- Smith goes into detail about the various benefits of each type of seafood he recommends

Squash

- Carrots, eggplant, cucumbers, parsnips, and zucchini are all approved for the Clean 20

- Squash is not a nutrient powerhouse, but is still a healthy addition to your diet as it is rich in fiber and low in calorie density

- Versatile for cooking; squash can be baked, grilled, roasted, sautéed, pureed, boiled, mashed and accompanies many different dishes, or can stand on its own

Sweet Potatoes & Yams

- Sweet potatoes are more nutritious than regular white potatoes, with higher vitamin content and a lower glycemic index

- They are lower in calories than their white counterparts and also possess anti-inflammatory properties

Tomatoes

- Alpha- and beta-carotene, lutein, and lycopene are four antioxidants that make tomatoes such a powerhouse

- Eating tomatoes with healthy fats like olive oil can double your body's absorption of crucial antioxidants

- Tomatoes are jammed full of lots of other vitamins and minerals too like vitamins A, C, and K along with potassium, copper, and magnesium

Turkey

- Rich in selenium, which is essential for proper thyroid and immune function

- Just because a meat says it's made from turkey doesn't mean it's healthy—read the ingredients on any "turkey ham" or "turkey bacon"

Whole Grain Bread

- Anything other than 100% whole wheat or 100% whole grain is strictly forbidden

- If bread just says, "Whole Grain," not all of the grains are whole; it must say 100%

- Check your bread for added sugars—most store-bought loaves have them; avoid if possible, if not, minimize

- Just because a bread is brown, doesn't mean it's healthy

Whole Wheat Pasta

- Barley, brown rice, buckwheat, corn, farro, kamut, millet, oats, quinoa, and spelt are all grains used to make whole wheat pasta

- Don't just shop by color, be sure to read the word "whole" before any grain that's listed

Yogurt

- Yogurt contains animal proteins and calcium, but many yogurts also contain digestion-boosting probiotics

- Not all yogurts contain probiotics, make sure it has "active" or "live" cultures to help build your gut bacteria

- Sugar is a major issue with some yogurt brands—take your time and choose a low-sugar, low-sodium option

THE CLEAN 20 RULES

Smith is quick to point out that the "rules" surrounding the Clean 20 diet are not hard and fast. They are malleable and adjustable. He doesn't expect you to sit in your house for the next 20 days. Instead, he says the keys to success are preparation and planning. Be aware when you're going to be out of the house and where you might be eating. Keep the right snacks in your car or at work.

The following rules will be your guide through your 20-day plan.

Dairy is Good. Despite what many fad diets are saying, and the seeming rise of lactose intolerance, dairy is good for you and is an important part of giving your body what it needs. Potassium and calcium are abundant in dairy, just be careful with the fat content.

Alcohol is bad—avoid it. You may be aware that red wine has antioxidants and can have health benefits in moderation. Regardless, let your liver focus on processing toxins and cleansing your system rather than metabolizing alcohol.

Soda is far worse than alcohol and is the worst thing on this list. This rule cannot be bent or broken.

If you really need a sugar drink, you can have ONLY freshly squeezed juice. Nothing from concentrate, nothing that says "100% juice." Only freshly squeezed with no sugar added.

Instead of soda and alcohol and juice, you're going to be drinking water. So much water. Most people don't drink enough, and you are going to find out what it's like to be completely hydrated. You may be surprised how different you look and feel.

You must do your best to remove all added sugar from your diet. This may not quite be possible if you have limited options at your grocery store, but do the best you possibly can. Artificial sweeteners are on this list as well. No Equal, Splenda, or anything similar. You will be reading the ingredients on every item you purchase.

Fruits and vegetables are your friends. You are allowed to eat any fruits and vegetables, even if your list goes above 20.

No MSG. While MSG is generally considered safe, Smith recommends avoiding it due to current controversy around its effects. It will be labeled on packaging as monosodium glutamate.

Frying and eating fried foods is forbidden during your clean 20. You may cook food in a little bit of olive oil, but that's it.

White flour is not allowed. As already discussed, Smith is highly focused on the nutritional benefits of 100% whole grain flour. Processed white flour has been stripped of all its nutritional benefits—making it similar to sugar in the way your body processes it.

Ketchup, mustard, salsa, and mayonnaise are allowed, but be careful. Smith advises to make your own condiments at home to avoid the added sugars found in store-bought brands. If you must purchase a condiment, be sure it is organic and does not contain added sugars.

If buying canned or frozen foods, be diligent to check the labels for added sugars, sodium, and preservatives. Canned goods should be kept only in water or natural juices. Look for "flash frozen" vegetables which can actually contain more nutrients than their "fresh" counterparts in the produce section, which tend to lose nutrients during shipment and storage.

Salad dressing should be made at home. If this is not possible, only organic dressing, without added sugar or artificial ingredients, is permitted.

HOW THE CLEAN 20 WORKS

During the 20-day program, try to be creative with the foods you're making. Prepare a variety of different snacks and meals each day as you experiment with what works best. Branch out and try foods you've perhaps never tried before like quinoa or spelt. Experiment with different spices. If you want to eat more than 20 foods, you can, so long as they fit into the original guidelines.

Key Takeaway: A daily meal plan will help control diversity and over-consumption

Each day, you will need to make a daily meal plan for yourself. While Smith provides plenty of recipes and options, you are also free to be creative and invent your own. Having variety in your plan will keep things interesting, keep you from getting bored, and diversify the nutrients your body is getting.

Along with your meal plan should be a level of portion control. This is not a calorie-counting diet and generally speaking, you can "overeat" vegetables as much as you want. However, learning portion control is an essential part of eating healthy, no matter what's on your plate.

Key Takeaway: Write down your Clean 20 to keep track of your variance.

You don't just want to eat some of the Clean 20, you want to eat them all. As you make your meal plans, put a check mark next to each food you're utilizing. This will help you to keep track of how much you're including each ingredient, and when you need to reincorporate one you may have forgotten about.

Key Takeaway: There is no rule for how to time your meals.

While Smith suggests a hearty breakfast and lunch along with a lighter dinner, he assures the reader that these choices are up to them. If you have plans to go out to dinner, try to adjust the rest of your day accordingly. He also suggests eating breakfast no more than 90 minutes after you get up, and lunch no more than three hours after breakfast. You should also avoid eating within 90 minutes of going to bed.

WHAT DOES THE CLEAN 20 LOOK LIKE?

Smith provides a detailed, daily meal plan for all 20 days including recipe suggestions, exercise requirements, and possible substitutions for most recipes. To access complete meal plans, please purchase a copy of the original book. Each daily plan contains the following:

Breakfast

Snack

Lunch

Snack

Dinner

Snack (if desired)

Let's Get Physical – Your daily exercise regimen

Food for Thought – A short blurb about the benefits of one of the Clean 20 Foods

Key Takeaway: Planning and preparation are necessary for success with the Clean 20.

If you don't plan out your meals and shop in advance, the Clean 20 is never going to work. Your fridge needs to be full of the healthy, approved foods that you will be cooking. If you don't have the right foods when hunger strikes, you will end up grabbing something quick on the way to work or worse—eating from the vending machine.

Key Takeaway: Each of the 20 days is focused on a different theme to help empower you and keep you motivated.

RESET: Just because you've failed at a diet in the past, does not mean you will fail at this one. Start with the belief that today is a new day.

EXPECT: Setting realistic expectations is critical for your success in anything. If you falter in your diet, don't worry, and don't give up.

BELIEVE: While you should be realistic in your goals, you have to have faith in yourself that you can achieve this. If you go in believing that you won't make it, you certainly won't.

PREPARE: Think ahead each day about what you're going to eat and what exercises you need to do. If you leave it until the last minute, you're only lessening your chances of success.

FOCUS: Start each morning by focusing on what you need to eat and do the rest of the day. Not only that, you must *maintain* focus throughout the day. Everyone is different, but learn what helps you best stay focused on your goals.

CLEANSE: The Clean 20 isn't just about cleansing your body for 20 days, it's about cleansing your life. Clean out the junk food from your cupboards; don't just promise yourself you won't eat it. Reduce your exposure to negative people and situations as much as possible.

VISUALIZE: Imagine all the incredible things that are happening inside your body as you enter the Clean 20. Imagine the clearer, brighter skin, the weight loss, the improved energy you will have. Visualizing helps us make our desires a reality.

ENJOY: Don't take things too seriously and don't let this diet become a chore. Part of the Clean 20 is learning to love new foods and the way they make you feel. Even if you encounter setbacks, laugh it off and remain positive.

BALANCE: All of life is about balance. There will be days it was impossible to get all your clean meals in, or when you simply couldn't exercise. Know that it's OK; keep everything in perspective.

ORGANIZE: Beyond cleansing your body, use this time to organize your life. Clean out your closet, start writing more things down. The more organized you are in your life, the better chance you have at success.

PUSH: Take the midpoint of the diet as a chance to look back on your progress. Be proud of what you've accomplished, but don't become complacent. Push harder.

DECELERATE: Take more time to enjoy life, to enjoy the wonderful foods you're eating, and to enjoy the positive changes you're making.

MOVE: While Smith provides daily exercises in his diet plan, they aren't set in stone. He encourages you to move as much as possible, in whatever way works best for you.

RELAX: It's critical to stay relaxed as you work through this plan. Stress has numerous negative effects on our bodies and should be avoided if at all possible. Take a deep breath. Everything is gonna be alright.

EXPERIMENT: Fight the urge to be a creature of habit and branch out—not just with your meal planning, but with travel and exercise. Variety opens new doors and keeps things interesting.

RESTORE: You can never underestimate the restorative power of sleep. Prioritize your sleep schedule during these 20 days to maximize the healing benefits of the plan.

INTRODUCE: Don't just change your diet, change your life. Introduce yourself to new people and things who will help you stay on the right course. In a similar vein, cut ties with those who are unsupportive of the changes you're making.

LEAD: It can be a rewarding experience to positively influence another person. Allow your journey and experience to be an example to those around you.

APPRECIATE: Focus on what you *do* have, not what you lack, in order to increase happiness. Be grateful for every modicum of progress you make, rather than begrudging every slip-up.

THRIVE: Don't let these 20 days stop here! Take everything you've learned and move forward. You don't have to perfectly follow the Clean 20 every day, but the better you can do, the more your body will thrive.

AFTER THE CLEAN 20

Once you finish your 20 days, it is critical to take stock of your successes and failures. Did you simply follow the rules, or did your mindset change throughout the process? Note what ways specifically your body feels better. How many times did you lapse? Do you think you could try it again? The Clean 20 isn't all or nothing; the more you can stick to it, the better.

Key Takeaway: Be careful in managing your reintroduction to processed foods.

Without question, you missed some foods during the Clean 20. And it is expected you will indulge in some French fries, a burger, or a glass of wine once you finish. But there are some foods on the "no" list that should never come back such as donuts, soda, and potato chips. Now that you have taught your body what it's like to be clean, it may not feel very good filling yourself with processed, sugar-laden foods. For the ones you do reintroduce, do it slowly.

Key Takeaway: Find substitutions to replace your least healthy habits.

If you were addicted to soda before the Clean 20, you may have found that flavored fizzy water was a good substitute. If you craved a cookie, maybe the sugars in a pineapple or pomegranate were enough to satiate your craving. Ideally, after the Clean 20 you won't fall immediately back on your old habits, but will have found healthy ways around them. If you immediately revert to eating sugary foods, you may need to reevaluate your motivations.

Key Takeaway: Cooking is the only way to truly manage what you eat.

While Smith encourages those following the diet to go out to restaurants and not put their life on hold for 20 days, he also admits that cooking at home is the only way to really know what's going into your food. Store-bought meals are often laden with sodium and seldom meet the criteria for "clean" and "unprocessed." While restaurants often use fresh ingredients, it is impossible to know how much oil or butter is being used in a dish that may be healthy when you eat at home. The answer is usually "a lot."

If cooking isn't something you're comfortable with, then now is the time to start! Don't take yourself too seriously and give some of the simpler recipes a try. You might surprise yourself!

RECIPES, SNACKS, AND EXERCISES

Smith provides step-by-step recipes and exercise to help you cook and move your way through the 20-day program. To access these recipes, snacks, and exercise guides, you will need to purchase a copy of the original book. In order to give you an idea, provided is a sampling of the titles of some recipes included:

Breakfast includes a Clean Green Smoothie, Baby Spinach Omelet, and Energy Explosion Yogurt. There are 12 breakfast recipes in total.

Lunch includes options such as Whole Wheat Spaghetti with Edamame Pesto Gusto, Succulent Turkey Burger, and Georgia Peach Salmon. There are 18 recipes in total.

Dinner focuses much more closely on seafood recipes, with choices like Sea Bass and Mango Salsa, Creole Salmon, and Cod with Zucchini Salsa. There are 16 recipes in total.

In addition, he provides recipes for making your own condiments and salad dressings at home—a step he believes is essential in avoiding the additives and sugars found in store-bought brands.

Throughout the book, Smith repeatedly mentions that these recipes—and his "version" of the Clean 20—are only suggestions. If you already love to cook and have recipes of your own, feel free to use them, so long as they abide by the rules. If you're new to cooking, but these recipes don't interest you, browse the internet for something that does.

Creativity is highly encouraged to help keep you motivated. If you don't like a certain recipe, keep looking around and playing with spices until you find something you love.

Smith stresses on multiple occasions the power of spices. Flavor doesn't always have to come from fat. Garlic, cumin, turmeric, coriander, oregano, chili flakes, and even just salt and pepper can change the way you think about food. Most importantly, healthy, clean food doesn't have to be bland.

EDITORIAL REVIEW

Ian Smith's diet-nutrition-exercise-motivation book is a simple, easy-to-follow, well-written guide to his Clean 20 plan. The book is laid out in a logical manner, first introducing the reader to the problems with highly processed diets, and then explaining the benefits in detail of each of the 20 foods he suggests. Smith goes as far as reviewing different varieties of each vegetable you might find in your local grocer, along with a comparative analysis of their nutritional values. While some of his tips for shopping for various produce are quite helpful—such as how to tell if an avocado is ripe and when to buy it—others are less revelatory, such as staying away from chicken with a "strong, unpleasant odor."

His diet and exercise plans are as specific as possible for those who need rigid guidance, but allow for experimentation, creativity, and substitution for those who don't. It is clear that Smith understands a great number of people fail at diets without flexibility, and, as such, he has created one with a higher chance of success for more people.

One of the greatest strengths of the Clean 20 is its diversity. Many fad diets today insist that gluten, dairy, or processed foods must be removed completely. Instead, Smith recognizes the benefits of a balanced diet including both bread and cheese: two staples of almost every American meal. He also admits that cutting out all processed foods can be close to impossible. Allowing those following the plan to still enjoy some things they love, albeit as part of a much healthier meal, offers a much greater chance of success for those making the biggest changes.

If you're already a generally healthy eater, there won't be much surprising news in here (added sugar is bad, vegetables are good), but the concept of the Clean 20 in itself is a worthwhile endeavor no matter how healthy or unhealthy your current lifestyle is.

BACKGROUND ON AUTHOR

Ian K. Smith, M.D. is an American physician who is best known for his appearances on the VH1 program, *Celebrity Fit Club*. He has also appeared on the *The View* and as a correspondent for NBC News. He has made smaller appearances on *The Tyra Banks Show*, *Larry King Live*, *Anderson Cooper 360*, and *Rachael Ray Show* among others.

Dr. Smith has been featured in *Time, Newsweek, Men's Health*, and the *New York Daily News*, and many other prominent publications. He received his bachelor's from Harvard, his master's from Colombia, and his medical degree from the University of Chicago Pritzker School of Medicine.

In 2007, Dr. Smith launched the national 50 Million Pound Challenge in order to help more Americans take control of their lives, their health, and their weight.

To date, he has written thirteen books.

OTHER TITLES BY IAN K. SMITH, M.D.

The Take-Control Diet (2001)

The Fat Smash Diet (2006)

Extreme Fat Smash Diet (2007)

The 4 Day Diet (2009)

Happy: Simple Steps to Get the Most Out of Life (2010)

EAT: The Effortless Weight Loss Solution (2011)

Shred: The Revolutionary Diet (2012)

The Truth About Men: The Secret Side of the Opposite Sex (2012)

Super Shred: The Big Results Diet (2013)

The Shred Diet Cookbook (2015)

The Shred Power Cleanse (2015)

Blast the Sugar Out! (2017)

The Clean 20 (2018)

END OF BOOK SUMMARY

*If you enjoyed this **ZIP Reads** publication, we encourage you to purchase a copy of the original book from.*

We'd also love an honest review on Amazon.com!

Made in the USA
Monee, IL
14 February 2022